NO FOREIGNER ONLY FAMILY

Abhijit Naskar is the twenty-first century Neuroscientist whose contributions in Cognitive and Behavioral Neuroscience have helped the world tackle the issues of mental illness, prejudice, hate, extremism, discrimination and segregation more effectively. As an untiring advocate of mental health and universal acceptance, he became a beloved best-selling author all over the world with his very first book "The Art of Neuroscience in Everything". With his pioneering ventures into the Neuropsychology of beliefs and biases, he has hugely contributed in the eradication of religious and cultural differences in our world, for which he is popularly hailed as a humanitarian scientist, who takes the human civilization in the path of sweet general harmony.

NO
FOREIGNER
ONLY
FAMILY

ABHIJIT NASKAR

No Foreigner Only Family

An Amazon Publishing Company, 1st Edition, 2020

Printed in the United States of America

ISBN: 9798656974356

Build Bridges not Walls: In the name of Americana
The Constitution of The United Peoples of Earth
Lives to Serve Before I Sleep
When Humans Unite: Making A World Without Borders
All For Acceptance
Monk Meets World
Mission Reality
Citizens of Peace: Beyond The Savagery of Sovereignty
Operation Justice: To Make A Society That Needs No Law
See No Gender
The Gospel of Technology
Every Generation Needs Caretakers: The Gospel of
Patriotism
Aşkanjali: The Sufi Sermon
Mad About Humans: World Maker's Almanac
When Call The People: My World My Responsibility

DEDICATION

*For every single person who's fighting for
Black Lives Matter*

CONTENTS

1. Preamble

Love not Allegiance
(A Sonnet)

If I am remembered O Soldier of Destiny,
Remember me with love not allegiance.
If you place me on the altar of your heart,
Make it not exclusive but exude acceptance.
When the darkness around bothers you,
Bask all you want in my timeless light.
But when you see others in darkness,
Forget your needs and serve with delight.
My heart will never leave your backbone,
So long as you have a cell crying for others.
I will receive honor and my highest reward,
When you annihilate yourself to wipe their tears.
I will keep burning through you for eternity,
Your actions will herald the victory of humanity.

ABHIJIT NASKAR

2. Adopting Society

I am the society, the society is me - this is the foundation stone of a civilized world. But at this very moment, these are mere words - a bunch of syllables stuck together. They are absolutely meaningless unless you feel them in the depths of your backbone. Truth not realized is truth wasted. You will know the truth when you become the truth.

So to build a civilized society mere book learning won't do, you must become one with society through every molecule in your body. So long as you and society are separate, troubles of the society will only multiply, but the moment you and society become one, those troubles will begin to drop, because oneness breeds responsibility and responsibility breeds solution.

Society is not just a word, it's a realization. Without this realization the very existence of humankind as a sapient species would turn into a myth. Harm done to the society is harm done to the self. But you can only feel this if you realize society in your veins, for through your veins flows the lifeblood of society.

Without the realization of society all knowledge brings out the worst in us, without us even being aware of it. Knowledge without a concern for others turns humans into savages - it does more harm than good. The worth of knowledge is to be measured based on whether it benefits others without discrimination. What good is your knowledge of five thousand books if it doesn't even help five people!

Use your knowledge to lift others - to lift the society. Destroy the self and place the society in its place. Rise up awakened by your humane fervor and announce to those around you - from this day forward I am adopting this neighborhood - the problems of each person in this neighborhood are now my problems - this day forward it's my responsibility to wipe the tears off your faces and turn them cheerful again.

Unless every cell in your body cries out in yearning - society, society, society - nothing good can ever happen to the world. Some may say, what about all the technological advancements that we have been making, don't they do good to the world! And my answer to this is - a world full of technological advancements but without a single caring heart, is more dead than alive.

In fact, that's the kind of world we've started to live in. Innovation after innovation after innovation, way beyond the actual necessity, has turned thinking humans into blind worshippers of technology. This way all we'll have left on this planet is technology, and humans will be mere extensions of those technologies that were initially invented to be extensions of the humans.

But mark you, technology is not at fault here, our recklessness is. Technology has no sentience of its own - it only follows our instructions. But what happens when we lose sight of the implications of that technology! Technology is the greatest feat of excellence that humankind has ever achieved, and I mean greatest, not one of the greatest, but the greatest, yet we have never truly understood the purpose of technology.

Hence, our own creation has now started to turn against us. Now, here I am by no means speaking against technology, I am merely pointing out its devastating implications that the vast majority of the population has remained blind to due to all the glare and glory of technology's beneficial aspects.

Without the soft and gentle hand of a human, no technology can ensure a healthy progress of humankind. Progress itself is meaningless, if in an attempt to get it, we lose all the sweetness of life. I am painstricken to say, today people value technology way more than they value a human. And if this continues, then we'll make progress alright, but that progress will hold no meaning to us.

Think about this a little. It takes merely a few months to build a fully functional humanoid robot, whereas Mother Nature took about 3.7 billion years to turn a single cell organism into a fully functional thinking and feeling human being. And how do we pay nature back - by acting all awestruck by the potential of machines while forgetting the worth of a human life around the corner. Shame on us! Are we this cheap and gullible!

Then there are other illusive human inventions that we have been paying more heed than human life - the invention of religion, the invention of race, the invention of nation, the invention of gender, the invention of intellectual supremacy, the invention of professional stature and so on.

It appears that humans value everything in the world except human life. But even if the whole human population start acting this way, which most of them do, we simply cannot accept it as mere human nature - we must do everything in our capacity to change that nature - yes, you heard right - we must do everything in our capacity to change that nature. Indifference to snobbery, bigotry and savagery turns them into the norm of a society – and only by standing up to such snobbery, bigotry and savagery, can we make sure that over time they lose their grip over the collective psyche of the society.

3. Life Lived for Others
(A Sonnet)

Life Lived for Others
(A Sonnet)

Torrents of joy have brought me salvation,
Bearing jewels of inclusion and unification.
My mind and my whole being have gone lost,
Into the rising tides of humanizing assimilation.
Finally serenity has arrived at my doorstep,
When I opened I found the bridge to others.
Defying all agony and selfish insecurities,
I discovered the supreme sentience in their cheer.
Their joy is my joy and their worry is my worry,
It is my vow upon the sacred pyre of conscience.
I stand ready to become dust if it is needed,
I am my gift to them, their smiles my recompense.
There is no point in living for the shallow desires,
Cause life is not lived till it's lived for others.

4. Parenting Society

Where a human values a human, there flourishes civilization - not religion, not race, not gender, not nation, not intellect, not profession, not anything else - human first, then everything else. And in such a civilization, there is no place for indifference. If a human in your neighborhood looks down on another human, it is your business - if a human in your surroundings discriminates a person, it is your business - if a human in your vicinity bullies another human being, it is your business.

The only reason discrimination, condescension and bullying still prevail in our society and that too at such glaring intensity, is because most people think these things are none of their business. They just see something like that happen on the street and simply walk away without uttering a single word. And silence of each human pumps fuel into the funeral pyre of humanity.

The moment the human in the humans wakes up nudged by their own active conscience, and begins to accept no more nonsense from bigots, racists and bullies, occurrences of inhumanity would start to drop exponentially. Each human must turn into a ravager of segregation, a purifier of prejudice and a destroyer of discrimination, only then will the human civilization receive salvation from the deathtrap of indifference induced inhumanity.

Here some may say, doesn't this sound a little violent! To them I say, the ravaging, purifying and destroying have nothing to do with violence. Considering silence to be nonviolence is a sign of our downfall, not progress. Strength used for oppression is violence, strength used for defending the weak is justice. It all comes down to one simple act - the act of not staying silent - not staying indifferent. Roar with conscience wherever you see inhumanity, and whenever someone even dreams of acting inhuman, one thought will haunt them day and night - don't you dare being inhuman, or else the ravager will come.

When each corner of the world has a handful of such ravagers, no inhumanity shall dare to raise its foul head. When I said in my previous works, "my world is my responsibility", I referred to all of the world, not just the good and humane part. The humane part of the world is my responsibility, as well as the inhuman part. It's all my responsibility - it's the responsibility of anybody with an unbending dignity and uncompromisable conscience.

Hence, it's the responsibility of the humans to keep the inhumanity of this world under control, just like it's the responsibility of the parent to bring their bully child under control. When a son exudes kindness, a great deal of credit goes to the parent (or parents), but at the same time, when a son misbehaves in the society, the blame for that too goes to the parent.

The blame for each inhumanity falls on each conscientious human. Think of the savage in your society as your spoiled child and step up as a concerned and conscientious parent to discipline the child. Remember, a bigoted president is your child that must be disciplined - a prejudiced cop is your child that must be disciplined - a reckless celebrity is your child that must be disciplined.

Let me tell you a story. A long time ago, when I first went up on stage to deliver a talk in front of some pretty influential people, my father asked me after the event, *"weren't you afraid to speak in front of all those bigshots"*, to which I replied, *"are you ever afraid to speak in front of me - then how can*

I be afraid of speaking in front of them, when I consider them all my children".

I chose to take the weight of the world on my shoulders, but you don't necessarily have to. If you can't take the weight of the world on your shoulders, take the weight of your nation - if you can't take the weight of your nation, take the weight of your city - if you can't take the weight of your city, take the weight of your neighborhood. Start small but start somewhere - take responsibility for the issues of your immediate vicinity if not the whole world, and the world will change, slowly but surely.

People need your courage - your conscience - your wisdom, never doubt it. They may not admit it, for they themselves do not know it, but they need you badly, as badly as the land struck by drought craves for rain – as badly as a ship lost in sea yearns for land. So, break your silence - break your apathy - break your nonchalance - and speak up. Speak up, for your silence is power to the savages. In fact, silence in front of savagery is savagery itself. Be not a savage my friend and speak up as a human.

A lot is hanging on that title "human". Do not make it a subject of ridicule for the humans yet to come. When those future humans look back at their ancestors, they ought to see brave beings of conscience and character, not some ragged and coward sheep in human's clothing.

5. Only Messiah is You

Ours is not an ideal world - no organic world can ever be ideal, that is, it can never be a utopia, but that doesn't mean we should cease all struggles for upliftment, because the moment we do, is the moment we get back down to the level of animals - or perhaps I should say, if we cease our struggles for upliftment and keep living a life of indifference and complacency, then we'd never rise above the animals.

To rise above the animals, we must be better than the animals. And the best way to be better than the animals is to sacrifice in the service of others, or at the very least, live life with a genuine concern for the wellbeing of others. Be prepared to die for the people and even in death you shall live. It's not how long you live that matters, but what you do with that life. Life itself is meaningless unless you put that life to some good use - some use that not only facilitates your own growth but that of those around you as well.

Life is not life till it comes to the use of others. This is the very foundation of true human existence. We are not born with the most advanced brain in the entire animal kingdom so that we could keep living like animals, selfishly obsessed with the needs of our own - we are born with it so that we could use it to lift others - we are born with it so that we could become the very epitome of conscience, character and assimilation.

Assimilation may sound like yet another concept of the philosophy books, but if you think of it that way, then I'm painstricken to say that our children are headed for catastrophe. Without assimilation, there is no hope for progress - without assimilation there is no hope for upliftment - without assimilation there is no hope of serenity. Hence, you must feel the force of assimilation in your very cells - in short, you must become assimilation yourself.

But mind you, no assimilation can come to life from a weak mind - strength is quintessential. Uncorrupt acceptance and unbending strength are the key to assimilation. However, do not confuse strength with lack of weakness. Strength doesn't mean absence of weakness, strength is the capacity to work through weakness. At times the weakness may feel overwhelming, but remind yourself this, on the other side of weakness lie the jewels of growth.

Weakness is good, it makes us humble. So, don't loath your weakness, rather accept it as a normal and healthy part of life, and in acceptance of weakness will rise the strength to work through that weakness. Weakness is a part of you, you are not a part of weakness. This means that you own your weakness, your weakness doesn't own you.

Weakness is yours to command, strength is yours to command - evil is yours to command, goodness is yours to command - you are the king of your own kingdom, so conquer your fears and weakness, for you are the messiah that is on demand. There is no other messiah but the human self. In you is the hope, in you is the sanity, in you is justice, in you is equality.

The world is filled with people who act good to gain recognition, but civilization is built on the shoulders of those who work for the good of all even when there is no witness. The shallow seeks witness of their good deeds, but those with character seek only to do good with their deeds. Be the witness to your own deeds, and no criticism will have power over you. Criticisms affect those who work for praise, but those who work for the pleasure of the work, are the living embodiment of stoicism. Praise them, mock them, it does not matter, what matters is that the work must go on, for there are lives to lift and faces to light up.

6. Salutation (The Sonnet)

Salutation
(The Sonnet)

My salutation to you O Human,
One who has broken the ties of creed.
The light was always within you,
Destroying the dogmas you set it free.
When your heart is labeled,
The world stays hypnotized in darkness.
The moment you rip them to pieces,
Tides of light awaken all synapses.
All separation is born of labels,
Tear those labels and there'll be light.
Once there is oneness in heart,
Oneness of humanity will manifest alright.
Emancipation lies in losing the I in Us,
Once you do, you will wake up the universe.

7. Oppression Breeds Revolution

Philosophy is useless if that philosophy doesn't improve the lives of the people - science is useless if that science doesn't improve the lives of the people - religion is useless if that religion doesn't improve the lives of the people. To put it simply, life is useless, if it doesn't improve the lives of others. Hence, injustice on one life is injustice on all lives - oppression of one life is oppression of all lives.

Oppression is the mother of revolution and revolution breeds justice, that is, if that revolution is driven by conscience, and not hate. Remember, there is a difference between an uprising against oppression and mob rule. And mob rule is as dangerous as tyranny, in fact, mob rule does more harm to a society than tyranny does, for even the tyrant uses some form of order to keep chaos out of the society, whereas when the very people turn into chaos themselves, with no more sense of justice than a bunch of hyenas, then the society goes backwards several centuries. So, it is imperative that all uprising be guided by an urge for justice, not a craving for revenge - the line between the two is extremely thin, but that very line separates a human world from the animal kingdom.

Basic instinctual drives have served us well, and keep serving the animals well, in the jungle, but in a civilized society these drives must never be given full control of our behavior, the moment we do, is the moment we fail ourselves. Remember, mob rule may appear to be justice at play, but it's only an illusion of justice. And illusion of justice is worse than injustice, for injustice is treatable with conscience but illusion of justice is untreatable, because those who play pretend justice are not even aware of the injustice they themselves are committing. They only replace the old injustice with a new one.

So, tread very carefully where injustice is concerned, because it takes very little for the oppressed to become the new oppressors. It is an extremely slippery slope. And though even the tyrant thinks that they are doing justice while committing injustice, an oppressor mob is far more dangerous than an oppressor tyrant. So, the people, the everyday ordinary people must never lose sight of their humanity.

In fact, if the people give rise to an uprising, it must be because of their humanity, not because of their savagery. And that's exactly what some of the most glaring movements of human progress are - a movement born of humanity - a movement of humanity. Black lives matter is not a black people's movement - metoo is not a women's movement - pride is not a gay people's movement - it's all humanity's movement - a movement for being accepted as humans by the humans.

8. Into The Eyes of Racism
(A Sonnet)

Into The Eyes of Racism
(A Sonnet)

I looked into the eyes of racism,
All I found was insecurity.
I looked into the eyes of prejudice,
All I found was pretend sanity.
I looked into the eyes of bigotry,
All I found was savage inanity.
I looked into the eyes of hate,
All I found was delusion of purity.
I looked into the eyes of disparity,
All I found was mindless conformity.
I looked into the eyes of apathy,
All I found was spineless vanity.
I looked a lot and observed plenty,
It's time to burn bright against brutality.

9. Beyond Belief and Intellect

We all have different tastes, hence, we have different paths, but this doesn't mean that any of those paths is superior to others - they simply are a part of a radiant, vivacious and diverse organic species. As long as a path is not founded on the oppression or belittling of others, it is a healthy psychological apparatus of the vast family called humankind.

A belief has no relation to the truth, nevertheless it is a quintessential part of human existence. In fact, there can be no human without belief. Machines run on facts and figures without the intervention of beliefs, but humans have not evolved in that way. In fact, even all of our advancements in the domain of facts and figures were caused by belief - by inkling - by hunch.

Here the intellectuals may say, what about reason? Does reason not have any role to play? Of course it does. Reason is as important as belief in the path of progress. But reason without belief (not to be confused with religious belief) leads to a harsh mechanical society and belief without reason leads to a discriminatory, prejudiced and barbarian society - only by working together can they pave the path of a healthy, sane and gentle progress. Progress alone won't do much good to humanity, it must be gentle, it must be healthy, it must be sane.

Let's conduct a thought experiment to observe this in detail. Imagine a world which is highly advanced - it has all the luxuries and comfort you can dream of in your wildest dreams - it has all the technologies that anybody can wish for - it has all the food that anybody would love to eat - it is a world without any limit to what you can possess - it has everything except one thing, joy. Now comes the quintessential question - would you be willing to live in such a world! I think you and I both know the answer.

But here is the harsh reality of the matter. That is exactly the kind of world we are heading towards, where humankind will have all the luxuries and comfort they can ever dream of, yet human life will lack the fundamental, uncompromisable element of joy. In fact, this has already begun to happen in the form of excessive consumerism. By excessive consumerism I am referring to consumerism beyond necessity.

Today, it has become a common trait of the people with affluence to buy things that they do not actually need, which is a subconscious attempt of the mind to fill in the scarcity of joy in their life with possessions. To put it simply. they are driven by a subconscious urge to fill the holes in their life with more possessions. And the more they possess, the more insecure they become, and the more insecure they become, the more they buy. It's an eternal death trap. And the only way out is to first distinguish necessity from luxury and then act upon that observation to not impulse buy anything that you do not actually need. And this is the very key to the joy that we have been missing in our life.

Advancement is not the problem, the real problem is us - we are our own enemy, for in most cases we are incapable of realizing the gravitas of the implications of the advancements that we accomplish. To look further, technology is not the enemy, capitalism is not the enemy, corporations are not the enemy, the enemy is everyday, ordinary human irresponsibility.

If the common human is responsible, then the world is bound to be humane, but if the common human is irresponsible, callous and indifferent, then no amount of protests and revolutions can eliminate inhumanity. Let me give you an example. One of the most obvious products of such indifference is the phrase "all lives matter", which has been used quite boastfully by so-called intellectuals from various corners of the world against the black lives matter movement.

The point is, on the outside the term "all lives matter" may sound quite intellectual and profound, but it is anything but that. It is not a product of profound observation - on the contrary, it is a product of lack of observation. Let me point out how. All lives matter is an intellectual luxury cooked up by couch philosophers, whereas black lives matter is an actual manifestation of the value of life through tangible human actions, which is moulding a world where all lives truly matter, not theoretically, but actually.

There is a difference between theory and practice - we may fill our heads with all sorts of pompous and luxurious theories, but they are not worth a penny unless you actually put them into practice. Using your luxurious theories to undermine actual human endeavors of justice and assimilation, only exposes the shallowness of your character.

And to those who pass comments from the sidelines, I say, if you can't assist in a movement for justice and equality, at the very least, don't undermine it. At the end of the day, a movement for justice and equality anywhere in the world benefits everyone everywhere in the world. And that is the reason, there is no such thing as black people's movement or women's movement or gay people's movement. One people's movement is all of humanity's movement.

10. Celebrating Colors
(A Sonnet)

Celebrating Colors
(A Sonnet)

Come my friend, it's time to color the world,
It's been vague and stale for eternity.
You and I, we all have the colors in us,
Why not use them to paint over all conformity.
Let's color with our words, thoughts and action,
So that not a single inch is left unrenovated.
Let's paint with justice, equality and sanity,
And make all offices of bigotry eliminated.
There is no lack of colors in the world,
Nor there is lack of determined conscience.
Once you recognize the colors in your heart,
The universe will rejoice in our united radiance.
Colors are plenty for us to celebrate together,
Hence we take a stand forging a humane future.

11. People Over Prejudice

A presumably insignificant movement in a little corner of your neighborhood has the power to revolutionize the fate of the entire world - so do not judge a movement based on its size, judge a movement if you must by the determination of its people. It's the determination of the people that adds power to the movement, not the other way around. Hence, if the people are willing and hell-bent to destroy the injustice and discrimination in their neighborhood, there is no power in the world that can stop them - even a thousand bigoted presidents with all the armed forces in the world would turn powerless in front of a hundred conscientious citizens hell-bent on justice.

What power has a president got, if the people stand up to his atrocities! The White House has authority over the people, so long as the people approve of that authority. The Whitehall has authority over the people so long as the people approve of that authority. The Kremlin has authority over the people, so long as the people approve of that authority. It's not enough to simply know and believe in the utopian concept that a government or law is supposed to serve the people - as a responsible "human" of the world, it is imperative that you practice that principle in your daily life to the letter and spirit.

Theories make good conversation pieces, but they are absolutely worthless unless the people are willing in their heart to put those theories in practice even if it means putting oneself in harm's way. If you are not ready to die fighting an injustice, your loved ones will die everyday because of that injustice.

Justice and injustice are both born of the mind, hence if the mind is determined to overwhelm every injustice with justice, nothing can stand in its way. It all depends on the will of the individual - it depends on you. No injustice is strong enough to face the wrath of the conscience determined for justice.

12. Determination Designs Destiny

There is no match for human determination in this whole wide world, so if you really want - and I mean really - truly – genuinely want, then you can do wonders - if you really, actually, genuinely want, you can end every single injustice in your neighborhood. Remember, justice doesn't mean absence of injustice, it means the presence of the determination to stand up to injustice.

Determination designs destiny, indifference invites doom. Break the indifference, be determined and march forward boldly fortified with accountability. Pay no heed to those who say you are weak - you are not weak, you are the master of your weakness. And once you master your own weakness, you would be able to master the weaknesses of the society.

So, master yourself and the society will mould itself as per your will. That's how advancement works - that's how progress works - it starts with the individual with a heart of honey and nerves of thunder. And when you rise as such an individual a thousand mountains would bow before you in veneration.

If you feel the miseries of the world, if you feel the injustice occurring daily in the world, if you feel the inhumanity that has crept into every corner of our society, then seek neither approval nor permission from anyone, instead awaken the human in you and stand up as a human.

What is justice, if not a basic sense of accountability! Justice doesn't come from books and institutions, it rises from the accountability of the ordinary human. I am using the term "ordinary human" to refer to every single regular person on earth, beyond stature and popularity, that is, I am referring to each one of us.

The stronger you cling to your armor of indifference, the more it strips you of your humanity. If you are okay with it, then by all means stay indifferent for the rest of your life, but remember this, every drop of your indifference turns into the ink with which you yourself write the doom of your own children.

Remember, if no one plants a tree today, people will not have a shade to sit in tomorrow. So, forgetting your selfish desire for reward and praise, you must plant a tree, knowing that you may not get to sit in its shade yourself - for this is real, actual, practical human existence. Unleash the human in you and to hell with consequences.

The problem of the society is, though it sees itself as a human society, it lives its whole life without ever unleashing the human within. They never unleash their conscience - they never unleash their empathy - they never let the petals of compassion and acceptance fully bloom. And till now, we may have somehow managed to live like this, but it can't go on any longer, for each day our inability or perhaps I should say our unwillingness to unleash the human in us makes the inhumanity around us more fierce and dominant. It's enough already.

The honor, integrity and serenity of this world are at stake here - the torch of human hopes is at stake here - so stand up and unleash the human. Remember the three fundamentals of progress - unity, faith and sacrifice. Be united as humans stepping beyond petty old tribalism - have faith in yourself and in humanity - and sacrifice all you can to design a humane tomorrow.

Turn yourself into such a self-evident torch of sacrifice that one call from you saying - "let there be light", will inspire others to hold their own lives up high as a symphony of light amidst the most traditional darkness. When darkness becomes tradition, someone must rise as the destroyer of that tradition. Never accept darkness as the norm, instead burn yourself to light up your society.

13.Other Side of This Sonnet

Other Side of This Sonnet

On the other side of this sonnet,
There is a land most bright.
In that land of inclusion and unity,
People are strolling without fright.
They walk, speak, run and play,
Without being accused of difference.
They celebrate life with love and delight,
In someone's need they rush in alliance.
Plenty though their paths may be,
Their sense of community has no label.
They have their differences surely,
Which makes them a species most able.
Now that we've arrived at the other side,
It's time we become that people forthright.

14.Movement Against Darkness

Darkness thrives on your silence - corruption thrives on your silence - tyranny thrives on your silence - break your silence and all darkness, all corruption, all tyranny will disappear - break your silence and the tyrants will wet themselves. No government, no party, no law, no army is stronger than the people - the resolve of the people can defeat even the strongest of armies - such is the power of the people - the people who are considered ordinary - the people who are considered common.

The resolve of a humble commoner can crumble a mountain to dust - what power does an injustice have in front of such resolve! It's all in your mind - you are oppressed as long as you approve of that oppression - the moment you learn to disapprove of that oppression, even centuries old oppression loses its ground.

My resolve is my strength - my conscience is my gospel - my action is my worship - thus speaks life - thus speaks liberty - thus speaks living humanity. For a long time humanity has remained desperately reliant on external authorities for even the most minuscule issues of life. And this reliance has turned a species of organic sentience into a species made of rigid nuts and bolts. Until we break this rigidity, prejudices and discriminations will keep festering in one form or another.

So, though it is necessary that we strengthen the movements against injustice and bigotry, alongside that it is also imperative that we continue our inner movement against the biases and prejudices inside our mind. And I beg you to not rush to the conclusion that you are free from biases and prejudices, for a living breathing human mind is biologically incapable of being free from biases and prejudices.

When each human joins the movement against their own prejudices, the prejudices of the world would begin to disappear sooner than you can imagine. When each human joins the movement against their own biases, the world would begin to be free from biases on its own.

Some may argue, how can a person standing up to their own biases free the world from biases! And the answer is rather simple, when you are aware of your biases and prejudices - when you have the guts to stand up to your own biases and prejudices, standing up to the biases and prejudices in your society would be first nature to you. And when standing up to the biases and prejudices in your society becomes your first nature, only then will there be hope for real, practical, genuine harmony on this planet.

15. The Supreme Salvation

Harmony is not ham sandwich sold across main street, you have to make it happen with your own two hands - with your blood and sweat and a whole lot of determination. It's not easy - it's never easy - nothing worth having in life is ever easy. Forget easy - forget hard - and just go out there and make it happen - make your resolve so strong that harmony, inclusion and acceptance would manifest out of your very nerve endings.

Leaders are not to reason why, leaders are to do or die. Die for your neighborhood - die for your society - die for your people - for our people - for our humankind. There is only one kind - humankind - there's no two way about it. So, forget all that "your kind my kind" nonsense, and just be kind. Kindness kindles kinship and kinship kindles a sense of community. When community and individuality become one, tyranny and oppression turn into history.

The strength of the community comes from the strength of the individual. Everything starts with the individual - with the self, so, it's always first the self, then everything else. But here by self I am not talking about self-obsession, rather I am talking about self-realization, not in a mystical and mythical sort of way, but in an everyday practical manner. Realize o mighty victors of destiny - realize your capacities - realize your ups and downs - realize your strength and your weakness - realize everything that you are - and from that realization will rise insight - insight to treat the sicknesses of our society.

To have eyes is useless, if your mind does not see. In fact, we do not see with our eyes, we see with our mind. Hence, when the mind is muggy, the world is muggy, and when the mind is clean, the world is clean. But the mind doesn't turn clean on its own, because we have inherited countless psychological impurities, savageries that is, from our evolutionary past.

We must be willing to recognize those impurities and overpower them with our civilized sense of conscience - once we do, all things selfish will disappear from earth, and we shall witness a world never seen before - where the self and the society will be synonymous and not separate. In such a world, self will be reflected in others and others will be reflected in the self. And this will lead you to the ultimate salvation.

Salvation will come through lifting others, not through reciting bible, quran or vedas. My society is my life - this should be on your mind day and night. Your own salvation lies in the salvation of your people. When the people smile, you smile - each smile caused by you is a reward of a lifetime – and there is no greater reward than this.

16. An Immigrant's Plight
(The Sonnet)

An Immigrant's Plight
(The Sonnet)

With hopes and dreams brimming in my heart,
I have traveled across miles and miles.
A single desire for a flame of acceptance,
Still burns bright in my heart's aisle.
You say home is where the heart is,
But my heart is accused of difference.
Sometimes I'm accused of faith or race,
Other times they question my allegiance.
Amidst the illusive fog of color and geography,
When did humanity cease mattering most!
Sentiments and dreams have no borders,
Character isn't exclusive to any single coast.
We've wasted enough time on labels and covers,
It's time to be family filling the world with colors.

17.In The Course
of Self-Determination

Human life is valuable, you know why, because it is the only form of life that is capable of working for the benefit of all, beyond the wildest imagination of all other lifeforms. So, live, not as a mere insect obsessed with desires of the self, but as a human, whose life finds meaning in coloring the lives of others. Remember, your power has no match in the world, so put that power to good use.

You may feel out of place sometimes, you may feel out of time sometimes – but mark this, it's not the place that makes the person, it's the person that makes the place. So, keep working - keep working through mockery, misery and desperation. Turmoil brings realization and realization brings discovery. So, fret not the turmoil, instead own that turmoil.

Announce my sisters and brothers at the top of your voice - the helpless, the hopeless, the forgotten, the discriminated, the alienated, the destitute are my family, and I will stop not till I lift them up to take their rightful place upon the fabric of society. The fabric of society is not crafted by the rich and privileged alone, it requires the heartfelt involvement of everyone. And if someone is not able to be involved in it, it is the existential duty of every conscientious human to come to the aid of that person and empower them until they become able.

But things are about to get a bit grey here, so please move slow. Helping people doesn't necessarily solve their problem for long - in such circumstances you need to help them but at the same time you must give them the tools for them to start helping themselves. Uplifting a people is much more than mere helping - uplifting a people is a combination of helping and empowering.

If you simply help them and assume that everything will be better for them now on, then you'd be making a grave mistake, because if people become too desperately reliant on your help and forget to solve the problems of their life on their own, then that's not progress, it's regress, so, though you must rush to the aid of those in need, your focus must always be on lifting them up to a position where they no longer need your help.

This is also the reason why the so-called concept of universal basic income (UBI) will create an unstable, lazy and reckless society. Give people universal basic jobs, not universal basic income, if you actually care for health, sanity and sustainable development of the society. Giving people money without any kind of labor on their part before they are mentally developed, creates a society of loyal, unstable, insecure subjects, not accountable, conscientious, free humans. And perhaps this is exactly what the figure heads advocating for UBI have in mind, that is, to create a perfectly non-thinking, mechanical society, ridiculously dependent on those figure heads.

It's one thing to support people in their daily life with welfare and other benefits and completely another to provide them money for life of which they don't know the value. Remember, the most effective way to control the people is to make them reliant on you through consistent reward with the least effort on their part. And if UBI is made a reality, it would be a great tool in controlling the lives and minds of the people.

The only way basic income can do real good to the society is if it is provided to those in need for a brief period of time, which could be two years to five years. I leave the final say on the duration to the economists. And let's call this revised form of basic income - limited period basic income (LPBI). To put it simply, limited period basic income can strengthen the preexisting welfare system in its efforts to empower the people and invoke equality, whereas universal basic income will only weaken the fabric of society and create deeper disparities.

A healthy, sane and sustainable society is where the state is responsible to support the people, but not to such an extent that the people become reliant on the state, and where the people are capable of taking care of themselves with minimum support from the state. Hence, become a power to the people, not a weakness. The moment they stop needing your help is the moment you succeed in your mission of truly helping them. Become self-reliant and help others to do the same. That's the greatest service you can ever do to the society. Self-determination is a fundamental ingredient of a healthy, honorable and progressive society.

No dignified human craves for charity, they only seek for the basic resources with which they can stand on their own two feet. Give them that if you can, and you'll be giving them life. The world needs your humanity, not your charity or pity. In fact, it's not the people who are fortunate that you are there to help them, but it's you who's fortunate to be of service to the people, for such is the highest use of your lifeforce.

18. Naked I Dance
(A Sonnet)

Naked I Dance
(A Sonnet)

Naked I dance here in delight,
I am not wearing name, fame or stature.
All I am wearing is a smile of humaneness,
Isn't that what matters in human nature!
I need no faith, nation or intellect,
Nor do I need illusive pomp and ceremony.
I am happy being a human above all,
I'll stay that way forever exuding harmony.
Tried a lot many countries, races and religions,
To tie me up with their rugged exclusivities.
But my heart is too grand for any one sect,
So I dance naked without any cultural amenities.
Come join me if you like my sisters and brothers,
United we'll free the world of all tribal attires.

19.To Step Beyond Inclusion

Even an animal can think of themselves, it takes a human to think of others. Only with such humans can we create an inclusive society, nay, only with such humans can we create a global family. It's not inclusion, it's humanity. The term inclusion is only a means to an end. But we must not lose sight of the goal, the mission - the mission of our entire species - and that is the mission to rise as one, united, undivided people.

Therefore, we must take the step beyond the term, and act as a manifestation of the meaning. We must act as living manifestations of assimilation. Accepting humans as humans is not inclusion, it's the ultimate emancipation - emancipation from the primitive shackles - emancipation from the savageries of our past - emancipation from the snobbery, egotism and bigotry of our ancestors - emancipation from the goody-goody illusive bounds of cultural, political, religious, intellectual and professional sectarianism.

Inclusion is not a philosophy - acceptance is not a philosophy - assimilation is not a philosophy - these are the backbone of human life. And what is life with without backbone! Kindness is not a philosophy - compassion is not a philosophy -

courage is not a philosophy - conscience is not a philosophy - are they!

All of this determines what it is to be human. You are alive - you are breathing - you are feeling the breeze - you are smelling the fragrance of the flowers - all these experiences have nothing to do whatsoever with philosophies - they are the fundamentals of life, likewise, inclusion, acceptance or assimilation, whatever you call it, is a fundamental of life. Without assimilation life's not worth calling human. Assimilation is the breath of life.

BIBLIOGRAPHY

Aristotle. Politics. Penguin; Revised, Reprint edition. (2000)

Aristotle. De Anima (On the Soul). Penguin Random House. 1987

Aristotle. Physics. Kessinger Publishing, 2004

Archer M., (2000), Being Human: The Problem of Agency. Cambridge University Press.

Archer M., (2003), Structure, Agency and the Internal Conversation. Cambridge University Press.

Adolphs R (2003) Cognitive neuroscience of human social behaviour. Nature Rev Neurosci 4: 165–178.

Adolphs R, Tranel D, Damasio AR (2003) Dissociable neural systems for recognizing emotions. Brain Cogn 52: 61–69.

Afton, A. D. (1985). Forced copulation as a reproductive strategy of male lesser scaup: A field test of some predictions. - Behaviour 92, p. 146-167.

Allison T, Puce A, McCarthy G. (2000) Social perception from visual cues: role of the STS region. Trends Cogn Sci 4: 267–278.

Andresen, Jensine, and Robert Forman, eds. Cognitive Models and Spiritual Maps. Bowling Green, Ohio: Imprint Academic, 2000.

Ashbrook, James, and Carol Albright. The Humanizing Brain: Where Religion and Neuroscience Meet. Cleveland, OH: Pilgrim Press, 1997.

Azari, Nina, Janpeter Nickel, Gilbert Wunderlich, Michael Niedeggen, Harald Hefter, Lutz Tellmann, Hans Herzog, Petra Stoerig, Dieter Birnbacher, and Rudiger Seitz. "Neural Correlates of Religious Experience."

European Journal of Neuroscience 13, no. 8 (2001)

Agar, N. (2004). Liberal eugenics: In defence of human enhancement. London: Blackwell Publishing.

Alteheld, N., Roessler, G., Vobig, M., & Walter, R. (2004). The retina implant new approach to a visual prosthesis. Biomedizinische Technik, 49(4), 99–103.

Antal, A., Nitsche, M. A., Kincses, T. Z., Kruse, W., Hoffmann, K. P., & Paulus, W. (2004a). Facilitation of visuo-motor learning by transcranial direct current stimulation of the motor and extrastriate visual areas in humans. European Journal of Neuroscience, 19(10), 2888–2892.

Bhat Z, Kumar, S, Bhat H (2015) In vitro meat production. Challenges and benefits over conventional meat production. J Sci Food Agric 14: 241–248

Bernstein R. J., (1967), John Dewey. New York: Washington Square Press.

Bernstein R.J., (1971), Praxis and Action: Contemporary Philosophies of Human Activity. Philadelphia: University of Pennsylvania Press.

Bernstein R.J., (1976), The Restructuring Social and Political Thought.

Bernstein R.J., (1983), Beyond Relativism and Objectivism: Science, Hermeneutics, and Praxis. Philadelphia: University of Pennsylvania Press.

Bernstein R.J., (1986), Philosophical Profiles. Philadelphia: University of Pennsylvania Press.

Bernstein R.J., (1991), New Constellation. Cambridge: MIT Press.

Barash, D. P. (1977). Sociobiology of rape in mallards (Anas platyrhynchos):

Responses of the mated male. - Science 197, p. 788-789.

Berger, J. (1986). Wild horses of the great basin: Social competition and population size. - The University of Chicago Press, Chicago.

Birkhead, T. R., Johnson, S. D. & Nettleship, D. N. (1985). Extra-pair matings and mate guarding in the common murre Uria aalge. - Anim. Behav. 33, p. 608-619.

Beauregard, Mario, and Vincent Paquette. "Neural Correlates of a Mystical Experience in Carmelite Nuns." Neuroscience Letters 405, no. 3 (2006)

Benson, Herbert. Timeless Healing: The Power and Biology of Belief. New York: Scribner, 1996

Bogen, J.E.(1995a), 'On the neurophysiology of consciousness: Part I. An overview', Consciousness and Cognition, 4.

Bogen, J.E. (1995b), 'On the neurophysiology of consciousness: Part II. Constraining the semantic problem', Consciousness and Cognition, 4.

Bremner, J. D., R. Soufer, et al. (2001). "Gender differences in cognitive and neural correlates of remembrance of emotional words." Psychopharmacol Bull 35 (3).

Brothers, L. (2002). The social brain: A project for integrating primate behavior and neurophysiology in a new domain. In J. T. Cacioppo et al. (Eds.), Foundations in neuroscience. Cambridge, MA: MIT Press.

Buss, D. D. (2003). Evolutionary Psychology: The New Science of Mind, 2nd ed. New York: Allyn & Bacon.

Buss, D. M. (1989). "Conflict between the sexes: Strategic interference and the evocation of anger and upset." J Pers Soc Psychol 56 (5).

Buss, D. M. (1995). "Psychological sex differences. Origins through sexual selection." Am Psychol 50 (3).

Buss, D. M. (2002). "Review: Human Mate Guarding." Neuro Endocrinol Lett 23 (Suppl 4).

Buss, D. M., and D. P. Schmitt (1993). "Sexual strategies theory: An evolutionary perspective on human mating." Psychol Rev 100 (2).

Blakemore SJ, Decety J (2001) From the perception of action to the understanding of intention. Nature Rev Neurosci 2: 561.

Bruce C, Desimone R, Gross CG (1981) Visual properties of neurons in a polysensory area in superior temporal sulcus of the macaque. J Neurophysiol 46: 369–384.

Buccino G, Vogt S, Ritzl A, Fink GR, Zilles K, Freund HJ, Rizzolatti G (2004) Neural circuits underlying imitation of hand actions: an event related fMRI study. Neuron 42: 323–34.

Colapietro V., (1988), "Human Agency: The Habits of Our Being." Southern Journal of Philosophy, XXVI, 2, pp. 153-68.

Colapietro V., (1992), "Purpose, Power, and Agency." The Monist, 75, 4 (October) pp. 423-44.

Colapietro V., (2003), "Signs and their vicissitudes: Meanings in excess of consciousness and functionality." Logica, Dialogica, Ideologica, a cure di Susan Petrilli e Patrizia Calefato (Milano: Mimesis), pp. 221-36.

Colapietro V., (2004a), "C. S. Peirce's Reclamation of Teleology." Nature in American Philosophy, ed. Jean De Groot (Washington, D.C.: Catholic University Press of America), pp. 88-108.

Colapietro V., (2004b), "Portrait of a Historicist: An Alternative Reading of

Peircean Semiotic." Semiotiche, 2/04 [maggio 2004], pp. 49-68.

Colapietro V., (2006), "Engaged Pluralism: Between Alterity and Sociality." The Pragmatic Century: Conversations with Richard J. Bernstein (Albany, NY: SUNY Press), pp. 39-68.

Colapietro V., (2009), "Habit, Competence, and Purpose." Forthcoming in The Transactions of the Charles S. Peirce Society. Calder AJ, Keane J, Manes F, Antoun N, Young AW (2000) Impaired recognition and experience of disgust following brain injury. Nature Neurosci 3: 1077–1078.

Carey DP, Perrett DI, Oram MW (1997) Recognizing, understanding and reproducing actions. In: Jeannerod M, Grafman J (eds) Handbook of neuropsychology. Vol. 11: Action and cognition. Elsevier, Amsterdam.

Carr L, Iacoboni M, Dubeau MC, Mazziotta JC, Lenzi GL (2003) Neural mechanisms of empathy in humans: a relay from neural systems for imitation to limbic areas. Proc Natl Acad Sci USA 100: 5497–5502.

Changeux JP, Ricoeur P (1998) La nature et la règle. Odile Jacob, Paris.

Cochin S, Barthelemy C, Roux S, Martineau J (1999) Observation and execution of movement: similarities demonstrated by quantified electroencephalograpy. Eur J Neurosci 11: 1839– 1842.

Chomsky Noam, (2017) Requiem for the American Dream

Chomsky Noam, (2016) Who Rules the World?

Chomsky Noam, (2010) How the World Works

Churchland, P.S. (1986), Neurophilosophy (Cambridge, MA: The MIT Press).

Churchland, P.S. & Ramachandran, V.S. (1993), 'Filling in: Why Dennett is wrong', in Dennett and His Critics: Demystifying Mind, ed. B. Dahlbom (Oxford: Blackwell Scientific Press).

Churchland, P.S., Ramachandran, V.S. & Sejnowski, T.J. (1994), 'A critique of pure vision', in Large- scale Neuronal Theories of the Brain, ed. C. Koch & J.L. Davis (Cambridge, MA: The MIT Press).

Crick, F. (1994), The Astonishing Hypothesis: The Scientific Search for the Soul (New York: Simon and Schuster).

Crick, F. (1996), 'Visual perception: rivalry and consciousness', Nature, 379.

Crick, F. & Koch, C. (1992), 'The problem of consciousness', Scientific American, 267.

Craig AD (2002) How do you feel? Interoception: the sense of the physiological condition of the body. Nature Rev Neurosci 3: 655–666.

Damasio, A (2003a) Looking for Spinoza. Harcourt Inc. Damasio A (2003b) Feeling of emotion and the self. Ann NY Acad Sci 1001: 253–261.

d'Aquili, Eugene. "Senses of Reality in Science and Religion." Zygon 17, no 4 (1982)

d'Aquili, Eugene. "The Biopsychological Determinants of Religious Ritual Behavior." Zygon 10, no. 1 (1975)

d'Aquili, Eugene. "The Myth-Ritual Complex: A Biogenetic Structural Analysis." Zygon 18, no. 3 (1983) d'Aquili, Eugene, and Andrew Newberg. The Mystical Mind: Probing the Biology of Religious Experience. Minneapolis: Fortress Press, 1999.

Daly DD. 1958. Ictal affect. Am J Psychiatry.

Damasio, A. (1994) Descartes' Error: Emotion, Reason and the Human Brain. New York, Putnams.

Damasio, A. (1999) The Feeling of What Happens: Body, Emotion and the Making of Consciousness. London, Heinemann.

Darwin, C. (1859) On the Origin of Species by Means of Natural Selection. London, Murray.

Darwin, C. (1871) The Descent of Man and Selection in Relation to Sex. London, John Murray.

Darwin, C. (1872) The Expression of the Emotions in Man and Animals. London, John Murray; also published

1965, Chicago, University of Chicago Press.

Dawkins, M.S. (1987) Minding and mattering. In C. Blakemore and S. Greenfield (eds) Mindwaves. Oxford, Blackwell, 151-60.

Dawkins, R. (1976) The Selfish Gene. Oxford, Oxford University Press; a new edition, with additional material, was published in 1989.

Dawkins, R. (1986) The Blind Watchmaker. London, Longman.

Di Pellegrino G, Fadiga L, Fogassi L, Gallese V, Rizzolatti G (1992) Understanding motor events: A neurophysiological study. Exp Brain Res 91: 176–80.

Deikman, A.J. (2000) A functional approach to mysticism. Journal of Consciousness Studies 7(11-12), 75-91.

Delmonte, M.M. (1987) Personality and meditation. In M. West (ed.) The

Psychology of Meditation. Oxford, Clarendon Press, 118-32.

Dennett, D.C. (1987) The Intentional Stance. Cambridge, MA, MIT Press.

Dennett, D.C. (1988) Quining qualia. In A.J. Marcel and E. Bisiach (eds) Consciousness in Contemporary Science. Oxford, Oxford University Press, 42-77.

Dennett, D.C. (1991) Consciousness Explained. Boston, MA, and London, Little, Brown and Co.

Dennett, D.C. (1995a) Darwin's Dangerous Idea. London, Penguin.

Dennett, D.C. (1995b) The unimagined preposterousness of zombies. Journal of Consciousness Studies 2(4), 322-6.

Dennett, D.C. (1995c) Cog: steps towards consciousness in robots. In T. Metzinger (ed.) Conscious Experience. Thorverton, Devon, Imprint Academic, 471-87.

Dennett, D.C. (1995d) The path not taken. Behavioral and Brain Sciences 18, 252-3; commentary on N. Block, On a confusion about a function of consciousness. Behavioral and Brain Sciences 18, 227.

Dennett, D.C. (1996a) Facing backwards on the problem of consciousness. Journal of Consciousness Studies 3(1), 4-6.

Dennett, D.C. (1996b) Kinds of Minds: Towards an Understanding of Consciousness. London, Weidenfeld & Nicolson.

Dennett, D.C. (1997) An exchange with Daniel Dennett. In J. Searle (ed.) The Mystery of Consciousness. New York, New York Review of Books, 115-19.

Dennett, D.C. (1998) The myth of double transduction. In S.R. Hameroff, A.W. Kaszniak and A. C. Scott (eds) Toward a Science of Consciousness: The Second Tucson Discussions and

Debates. Cambridge, MA, MIT Press, 97-107.

Dennett, D.C. (1998b) Brainchildren: Essays on Designing Minds. Cambridge, MA, MIT Press.

Dennett, D.C. (2001) The fantasy of first person science. Debate with D. Chalmers, Northwestern University, Evanston, IL, February 2001.

Dennett, D.C. (2003) Freedom Evolves. New York, Penguin.

Dennett, D.C. and Kinsbourne, M. (1992) Time and the observer: the where and when of consciousness in the brain. Behavioral and Brain Sciences 15, 183-247, including commentaries and authors' responses.

Dewey J., (1911 [1977]), "Epistemological Realism: The Alleged Ubiquity of the Knowledge Relation." Journal of Philosophy, VIII, 20 (September 28, 1911).

Dewhurst, Kenneth, and A. W. Beard. "Sudden Religious Conversions in Temporal Lobe Epilepsy." British Journal of Psychiatry 117 (1970)

Dewhurst K, Beard AW. Sudden religious conversions in temporal lobe epilepsy. 1970 Epilepsy Behav 2003

Devinsky O, Lai G. Spirituality and religion in epilepsy. Epilepsy Behav 2008.

Devinsky, O., Morrell, MJ, Vogt, BA. (1995) 'Contribution of anterior cingulate cortex to behavior', Brain, 118.

Douglas Stone A., Chapter 24, The Indian Comet, in the book Einstein and the Quantum, Princeton University Press, Princeton, New Jersey, 2013.

E. Horvitz, "One Hundred Year Study on Artificial Intelligence: Reflections and Framing," ed: Stanford University, 2014.

Einstein A. (1925). "Quantentheorie des einatomigen idealen Gases". Sitzungsberichte der Preussischen Akademie der Wissenschaften.

Eckhart Meister, Selected Writings

Egidi R., ed. (1999), "Von Wright and 'Dante's Dream': Stages in a Philosophical Pilgrim's Progress", in In Search of a New Humanism: the Philosophy of G.H. von Wright, ed. by R. Egidi, Kluwer, Dordrecht.

Fadiga L, Fogassi L, Pavesi G, Rizzolatti G (1995) Motor facilitation during action observation: a magnetic stimulation study. J Neurophysiol 73: 2608–2611.

Fogassi L, Gallese V, Fadiga L, Rizzolatti G (1998) Neurons responding to the sight of goal directed hand/arm actions in the parietal area PF (7b) of the macaque monkey. Soc Neurosci Abs 24:257.5.

Frith U, Frith CD (2003) Development and neurophysiology of mentalizing. Philos Trans R Soc Lond B Biol Sci 358: 459.

Farah, M.J. (1989), 'The neural basis of mental imagery', Trends in Neurosciences, 10.

Finlay BL, Darlington RB (1995) Linked regularities in the development and evolution of mammalian brains. Science 268.

Freud, S. "The Interpretation of Dreams", 1900

Freud, S. "Selected papers on hysteria and other psychoneuroses" Journal of Nervous and Mental Disease 1909.

Freud, S. "The Origin and Development of Psychoanalysis", 1910

Freud, S. "Psychopathology of everyday life", 1914

Freud, S. "Beyond the Pleasure Principle", 1920

Frith, C.D. & Dolan, R.J. (1997), 'Abnormal beliefs: Delusions and memory', Paper presented at the May, 1997, Harvard Conference on Memory and Belief.

Gay, Volney, ed. Neuroscience and Religion. Plymouth, UK: Lexington Books, 2009.

Gazzaniga, M. S. (1985). The social brain. New York: Basic Books.

Gazzaniga, M.S. (1993), 'Brain mechanisms and conscious experience', Ciba Foundation Symposium, 174.

Geschwind N. "Behavioural changes in temporal lobe epilepsy". Psychol Med. 1979.

Gellhorn, E., Kiely, W.F. "Mystical states of consciousness: neurophysiological and clinical aspects." J Nerv Ment Dis. 1972;154:399-405.

Gilbert SL, Dobyns WB, Lahn BT (2005) Genetic links between brain development and brain evolution. Nat Rev Genet 6.

Gray JA. The Psychology of Fear and Stress. 2nd ed. New York, NY: Cambridge University Press; 1988.

Gloor, P. (1992), 'Amygdala and temporal lobe epilepsy', in The Amygdala: Neurobiological Aspects of Emotion, Memory and Mental Dysfunction, ed J.P. Aggleton (New York: Wiley-Liss).

Greenspan, S. I. and S. G. Shanker (2004). The first idea: How symbols, language, and intelligence evolved from our early primate ancestors to modern humans. Cambridge, MA: Da Capo Press.

Grady, D. (1993), 'The vision thing: Mainly in the brain', Discover, June.

Gallagher HL, Frith CD (2003) Functional imaging of 'theory of mind'. Trends Cogn Sci 7: 77.

Gallese V, Fogassi L, Fadiga L, Rizzolatti G (2002) Action representation and the inferior parietal lobule. In: Prinz W, Hommel B (eds) Attention & Performance XIX. Common mechanisms in perception and action. Oxford University Press, Oxford.

Gallese V, Keysers C, Rizzolatti G (2004) A unifying view of the basis of social cognition. Trends Cogn Sci 8: 396–403.

Gangitano M, Mottaghy FM, Pascual-Leone A (2001) Phase specific modulation of cortical motor output during movement observation. NeuroReport 12: 1489–1492.

Gangitano M, Mottaghy FM, Pascual-Leone A (2004) Modulation of premotor mirror neuron activity during observation of unpredictable grasping movements. Eur J Neurosci 20: 2193– 2202.

Goldman AI, Sripada CS (2004) Simulationist models of face-based emotion recognition. Cognition 94: 193–213.

Grèzes J, Costes N, Decety J (1998) Top-down effect of strategy on the perception of human biological motion: a PET investigation. Cogn Neuropsychol 15: 553–582.

Grèzes J, Armony JL, Rowe J, Passingham RE (2003) Activations related to "mirror" and "canonical" neurones in the human brain: an fMRI study. Neuroimage 18: 928–937.

Gross CG, Rocha-Miranda CE, Bender DB (1972) Visual properties of neurons in the inferotemporal cortex of the macaque. J Neurophysiol 35: 96–111.

Hari R, Forss N, Avikainen S, Kirveskari S, Salenius S, Rizzolatti G

(1998) Activation of human primary motor cortex during action observation: a neuromagnetic study. Proc. Natl Acad Sci USA 95: 15061–15065.

Hardy, G. H. (1940). Ramanujan. Cambridge: Cambridge University Press.

Hall, Daniel, Keith Meador, and Harold Koenig. "Measuring Religiousness in Health Research: Review and Critique." Journal of Religion and Health 47, no. 2 (2008)

Harris, Sam, Jonas Kaplan, Ashley Curiel, Susan Bookheimer, Marco Iacoboni, and Mark Cohen. "The Neural Correlates of Religious and Nonreligious Belief." PLoS One 4, no. 10 (October 1, 2009)

Halgren, E. (1992), 'Emotional neurophysiology of the amygdala within the context of human cognition', in The Amygdala:

Neurobiological Aspects of Emotion, Memory and Mental Dysfunction, ed J.P. Aggleton (New York: Wiley-Liss).

Halligan PW, Fink GR, Marshal JC, Vallar G. 2003. Spatial cognition: evidence from visual neglect. Trends Cogn Sci.

Handbook of Emotions, Edited by Michael Lewis, Jeannette M. Haviland-Jones, and Lisa Feldman Barrett, The Guilford Press; 3rd edition (2010).

Haggard, P., Clark, S. and Kalogeras,]. (2002) Voluntary action and conscious awareness, Nature Neuroscience 5, 382-5. Haggard, P., Newman, C. and Magno, E. (1999) On the perceived time of voluntary actions. British Journal of Psychology 90, 291-303.

Hameroff, S.R. and Penrose, R. (1996) Conscious events as orchestrated space-time selections. Journal of Consciousness Studies 3(1), 36-53; also reprinted in J. Shear (ed.) (1997

Explaining Consciousness-The Hard Problem. Cambridge, MA, MIT Press, 177-95.

Hardcastle, V.G. (2000) How to understand theN in NCC. InT. Metzinger (ed.) Neural Correlates of Consciousness. Cambridge, MA, MIT Press, 259-64.

Harding, D.E. (1961) On Having no Head: Zen and the Re-Discovery of the Obvious. London, Buddhist Society.

Hardy, A. (1979) The Spiritual Nature of Man: A Study of Contemporary Religious Experience. Oxford, Clarendon Press.

Hamad, S. (1990) The symbol grounding problem. Physica D 42, 335-46.

Hamad, S. (2001) No easy way out. The Sciences 41(2), 36-42.

Harre, R. and Gillett, G. (1994) The Discursive Mind. Thousand Oaks, CA, Sage.

Haugeland, J. (ed.) (1997) Mind Design II: Philosophy, Psychology, Artificial Intelligence. Cambridge, MA, MIT Press.

Hauser, M.D. (2000) Wild Minds: What Animals Really Think. New York, Henry Holt and Co.; London, Penguin.

Hearne, K. (1990) The Dream Machine. Northants, Aquarian.

Hebb, D.O. (1949) The Organization of Behavior. New York, Wiley.

Helmholtz, H.L.F. von (1856-67) Treatise on Physiological Optics.

Hess, EH (1975) "The role of pupil size in communication," Scientific American, 233(5), 110–12.

Heyes, C.M. (1998) Theory of mind in nonhuman primates. Behavioral and

Brain Sciences 21, 101-48; with commentaries.

Heyes, C.M. and Galef, B.G. (eds) (1996) Social Learning in Animals: The Roots of Culture. San Diego, CA, Academic Press.

Hilgard, E.R. (1986) Divided Consciousness: Multiple Controls in Human Thought and Action. New York, Wiley.

Hocquette JF (2016) Is in vitro meat the

solution for the future? Meat Science 120:

167–176

Hodgson, R. (1891) A case of double consciousness. Proceedings of the Society for Psychical Research 7, 221-58.

Hofstadter, D.R. (1979) Code!, Escher, Bach: An Eternal Golden Braid. London, Penguin.

Hofstadter, D.R. and Dennett, D.C. (eds) (1981) The Mind's I: Fantasies and Reflections on Self and Soul. London, Penguin.

Holland, J. (ed.) (2001) Ecstasy: The Complete Guide: A Comprehensive Look at the Risks and Benefits of MDMA. Rochester, VT, Park Street Press.

Holmes, D.S. (1987) The influence of meditation versus rest on physiological arousal. In M. West (ed.) The Psychology of Meditation. Oxford, Clarendon Press, 81-103.

Holt, J. (1999) Blindsight in debates about qualia. Journal of Consciousness Studies 6(5), 54-71.

Horgan, J. (1994), 'Can science explain consciousness?', Scientific American, 271.

Holloway RL (1996) Evolution of the human brain. In: Lock A, Peters CR (eds) Handbook of human symbolic evolution. Oxford University Press, Oxford

Iacoboni M, Woods RP, Brass M, Bekkering H, Mazziotta JC, Rizzolatti G (1999) Cortical mechanisms of human imitation. Science 286: 2526–2528.

Iacoboni M, Koski LM, Brass M, Bekkering H, Woods RP, Dubeau MC, Mazziotta JC, Rizzolatti G (2001) Reafferent copies of imitated actions in the right superior temporal cortex. Proc Natl Acad Sci USA 98: 13995–13999.

Jeannerod M (1988) The neural and behavioural organization of goal-directed movements. Clarendon Press, Oxford.

Johnson-Frey SH, Maloof FR, Newman-Norlund R, Farrer C, Inati S, Grafton ST (2003) Actions or hand-objects interactions? Human inferior frontal cortex and action observation. Neuron 39: 1053–1058.

Jackson, F. (1982) Epiphenomenal qualia. Philosophical Quarterly 32, 127-36.

James, W. (1890) The Principles of Psychology (2 volumes). London, Macmillan.

James, W. (1902) The Varieties of Religious Experience: A Study in Human Nature. New York and London, Longmans, Green and Co.

Jansen, K. (2001) Ketamine: Dreams and Realities. Sarasota, FL, Multidisciplinary Association for Psychedelic Studies.

Jay, M. (ed.) (1999) Artificial Paradises: A Drugs Reader. London, Penguin.

Jaynes, J. (1976) The Origin of Consciousness in the Breakdown of the Bicameral Mind. New York, Houghton Mifflin.

Johnson, M.K. and Raye, C.L. (1981) Reality monitoring. Psychological Review 88, 67-85.

Kadim I, Mahgoub O, Baqir S et al. (2015) Cultured meat from muscle stem cells: a review of challenges and prospects. J Integr Agr 14: 222–233

Koski L, Iacoboni M, Dubeau MC, Woods RP, Mazziotta JC (2003) Modulation of cortical activity during different imitative behaviors. J Neurophysiol 89: 460–471.

Krolak-Salmon P, Henaff MA, Isnard J, Tallon-Baudry C, Guenot M, Vighetto A, Bertrand O, Mauguiere F (2003) An attention modulated response to disgust in human ventral anterior insula. Ann Neurol 53: 446–453.

Kandel, E. R. In Search of Memory: The Emergence of a New Science of Mind, W. W. Norton & Company (2007).

Kandel E. R. Schwartz JH, Jessel TM. Principles of neural sciences. New York; McGraw Hill, 2000.

Kanizsa, G. (1979), Organization In Vision (New York: Praeger).

Kaloupek DG, Scott JR, Khatami V. Assessment of coping strategies associated with syncope in blood donors. J Psychosom Res. 1985;29:207-214.

Kanwisher, N. (2001) Neural events and perceptual awareness. Cognition 79, 89-113; also reprinted inS. Dehaene (ed.) The Cognitive Neuroscience of Consciousness. Cambridge, MA, MIT Press, 89-113.

Kapleau, Roshi P. (1980) The Three Pillars of Zen: Teaching, Practice, and Enlightenment (revised edn). New York, Doubleday.

Karn, K. and Hayhoe, M. (2000) Memory representations guide

targeting eye movements in a natural task. Visual Cognition 7, 673-703.

Kasamatsu, A. and Hirai, T. (1966) An electroencephalographic study on the Zen meditation (zazen). Folia Psychiatrica et Neurologica Japonica 20, 315-36.

Kaiserman-Abramof, I. R., Graybiel, A. M., & Nauta, W. J. (1980). The thalamic projection to cortical area 17 in a congenitally anophthalmic mouse strain. Neuroscience, 5, 41–52.

Kanold, P. O., Kara, P., Reid, R. C., & Shatz, C. J. (2003). Role of subplate neurons in functional maturation of visual cortical columns. Science, 301, 521–525.

Kennedy, H., & Dehay, C. (1988). Functional implications of the anatomical organization of the callosal projections of visual areas V1 and V2 in the macaque monkey. Behav. Brain Res., 29, 225–236.

Kentridge, R.W. and Heywood, C.A. (1999) The status of blindsight. Journal of Consciousness Studies 6(5), 3-11.

Kihlstrom, J.F. (1996) Perception without awareness of what is perceived, learning without awareness of what is learned. In M. Velmans (ed.) The Science of Consciousness. London, Routledge, 23-46.

Kollerstrom, N. (1999) The path of Halley's comet, and Newton's late apprehension of the law of gravity. Annals of Science 56, 331-56.

Kosslyn, S.M. (1980) Image and Mind. Cambridge, MA, Harvard University Press.

Kosslyn, S.M. (1988) Aspects of a cognitive neuroscience of mental imagery. Science 240, 1621-6.

Kinsbourne, M. (1995), 'The intralaminar thalamic nucleii', Consciousness and Cognition, 4.

Kjaer, Troels, Camilla Bertelsen, Paola Piccini, David Brooks, Jorgen Alving, and Hans Lou. "Increased Dopamine Tone during Meditation- Induced Change of Consciousness." Cognitive Brain Research 13, no. 2 (April 2002)

Kölmel HW. 1985. Complex visual hallucinations in the hemianopic field. J Neurol Neurosurg Psychiatry.

Koenig, Harold. "Research on Religion, Spirituality, and Mental Health: A Review." Canadian Journal of Psychiatry 54, no. 5 (May 2009)

Koenig, Harold, ed. Handbook of Religion and Mental Health. San Diego, CA: Academic Press, 1998

Kraepelin E. Psychiatry: A Textbook for Students and Physicians. New York, NY: Science History Publications; 1990.

Lauglin, Charles, John McManus, and Eugene d'Aquili. Brain, Symbol, and

Experience. 2nd ed. New York: Columbia University Press, 1992

Lakoff, G. and M. Johnson (1999). Philosophy in the flesh. Basic Books: New York.

LeDoux, J. E. (1996). The emotional brain. New York: Simon & Schuster.

LeDoux, J.E. (1992), 'Emotion and the amygdala', in The Amygdala: Neurobiological Aspects of Emo- tion, Memory and Mental Dysfunction, ed J.P. Aggleton (New York: Wiley-Liss).

Levin, D.T. and Simons, D.J. (1997) Failure to detect changes to attended objects in motion pictures. Psychonomic Bulletin and Review 4, 501-6.

Levine,J. (1983) Materialism and qualia: the explanatory gap. Pacific Philosophical Quarterly 64, 354-61.

Levine,J. (2001) Purple Haze: The Puzzle of Consciousness. New York,

Oxford University Press. Levine, S. (1979) A Gradual Awakening. New York, Doubleday.

Levinson, B.W. (1965) States of awareness during general anaesthesia. British Journal of Anaesthesia 37, 544-6.

Lewicki, P., Czyzewska, M. and Hoffman, H. (1987) Unconscious acquisition of complex procedural knowledge. Journal of Experimental Psychology: Learning, Memory and Cognition 13, 523-30.

Lewicki, P., Hill, T. and Bizot, E. (1988) Acquisition of procedural knowledge about a pattern of stimuli that cannot be articulated. Cognitive Psychology 20, 24-37.

Lewicki, P., Hill, T. and Czyzewska, M. (1992) Nonconscious acquisition of information. American Psychologist 47, 796-801.

Manthey S, Schubotz RI, von Cramon DY (2003). Premotor cortex in observing erroneous action: an fMRI study. Brain Res Cogn Brain Res 15: 296–307.

Mesulam MM, Mufson EJ (1982) Insula of the old world monkey. III: Efferent cortical output and comments on function. J Comp Neurol 212: 38–52.

Naskar, Abhijit. "Homo: A Brief History of Consciousness", 2015

Naskar, Abhijit. "What is Mind?", 2016

Naskar, Abhijit. "In Search of Divinity: Journey to The Kingdom of Conscience", 2016

Naskar, Abhijit. "Love, God & Neurons: Memoir of A Scientist who found himself by getting lost", 2016

Naskar, Abhijit. "Neurons of Jesus: Mind of A Teacher, Spouse & Thinker", 2017

Naskar, Abhijit. "The Islamophobic Civilization: Voyage of Acceptance", 2017

Naskar, Abhijit. "Principia Humanitas", 2017

Naskar, Abhijit. "We Are All Black: A Treatise on Racism", 2017

Naskar, Abhijit. "Wise Mating: A Treatise on Monogamy", 2017

Naskar, Abhijit. "I Am The Thread: My Mission", 2017

Naskar, Abhijit. "The Bengal Tigress: A Treatise on Gender Equality", 2017

Naskar, Abhijit. "Build Bridges not Walls: In the name of Americana", 2018

Naskar, Abhijit. "Fabric of Humanity", 2018

Naskar, Abhijit. "Lives To Serve Before I Sleep", 2019

Naskar, Abhijit. "Citizens of Peace: Beyond the Savagery of Sovereignty", 2019

Naskar, Abhijit. "The Constitution of The United Peoples of Earth", 2019

Naskar, Abhijit. "Neurons Giveth, Neurons Taketh Away | Abhijit Naskar | TEDxIIMRanchi", 2019 https://www.youtube.com/watch?v=BNX-Q0ySm80

Naskar, Abhijit. "Mission Reality", 2019

Naskar, Abhijit. "Operation Justice: To Make A Society That Needs No Law", 2019

Naskar, Abhijit. "Every Generation Needs Caretakers: The Gospel of Patriotism", 2020

Naskar, Abhijit. "The Gospel of Technology", 2020

Naskar, Abhijit. "When Call The People: My World My Responsibility", 2020

Newberg, Andrew, and Jeremy Iversen. "The Neural Basis of the Complex Mental Task of Meditation: Neurotransmitter and Neurochemical Considerations." Medical Hypotheses 61, no. 2 (2003).

Newberg, Andrew. "How God Changes Your Brain: An Introduction to Jewish Neurotheology", CCAR Journal: The Reform Jewish Quarterly, Winter 2016.

Newberg, Andrew, and Stephanie Newberg. "A Neuropsychological Perspective on Spiritual Development." In Handbook of Spiritual Development in Childhood and Adolescence, edited by Eugene Roehlkepartain, Pamela King, Linda Wagener, and Peter Benson. London: Sage Publications, Inc., 2005

Newberg, Andrew. "The Neurotheology Link An Intersection Between Spirituality and Health", Alternative and Complimentary Therapies, Vol 21 No 1, February 2015.

Newberg, Andrew, Nancy Wintering, Dharma Khalsa, Hannah Roggenkamp, and Mark Waldman. "Meditation Effects on Cognitive Function and Cerebral Blood Flow in Subjects with Memory Loss: A Preliminary Study." Journal of Alzheimer's Disease 20, no. 2 (2010)

Nash, M. (1995), 'Glimpses of the mind', Time.

Nesse RM. Proximate and evolutionary studies of anxiety, stress and depression: synergy at the interface. Neurosci Biobehav Rev. 1999;23:895-903.

Nicolelis, Miguel. (2011) "Beyond Boundaries: The New Neuroscience of Connecting Brains with Machines---

and How It Will Change Our Lives", Times Books

O'Hara, K. and Scutt, T. (1996) There is no hard problem of consciousness. Journal of Consciousness Studies 3(4), 290-302, reprinted in J. Shear (ed.) (1997) Explaining Consciousness. Cambridge, MA, MIT Press, 69-82.

O'Regan, J.K. (1992) Solving the "real" mysteries of visual perception: the world as an outside memory. Canadian Journal of Psychology 46, 461-88.

O'Regan, J.K. and Noe, A. (2001) A sensorimotor account of vision and visual consciousness. Behavioral and Brain Sciences 24(5), 883-917.

O'Regan, J.K., Rensink, R.A. and Clark,].]. (1999) Change-blindness as a result of "mudsplashes." Nature 398, 34.

Ornstein, R.E. (1977) The Psychology of Consciousness (2nd edn). New York, Harcourt.

Ornstein, R.E. (1986) The Psychology of Consciousness (3rd edn). New York, Pehguin.

Ornstein, R.E. (1992) The Evolution of Consciousness. New York, Touchstone.

Penfield W, Faulk ME (1955) The insula: further observations on its function. Brain 78: 445– 470.

Penrose, R. (1994), Shadows of the Mind (Oxford: Oxford University Press).

Penrose, R. (1989), The Emperor's New Mind: Concerning Computers, Minds and The Laws of Physics (Oxford: Oxford University Press).

Persinger, "'I would kill in God's name' role of sex, weekly church attendance, report of a religious experience and limbic lability" Perceptual and Motor Skills 1997.

Persinger "Experimental simulation of the God experience" Neurotheology 2003.

Persinger, M. A. (1993b). Personality changes following brain injury as a grief response to the loss of sense of self: Phenomenological themes as indices of local lability and neurocognitive restructuring as psycho- therapy. Psychological Reports, 72

Persinger, Corradini, Clement, Keaney, et al "Neurotheology and its convergence with neuroquantology" NeuroQuantology 2010.

Persinger, Koren and St-Pierre "The electromagnetic induction of mystical and altered states within the laboratory" Journal of Consciousness Exploration and Research 2010.

Persinger "Case report: A prototypical spontaneous 'sensed presence' of a sentient being and concomitant electroencephalographic activity in the clinical laboratory" Neurocase 2008.

Persinger and Saroka "Potential production of Hughlings Jackson's "parasitic consciousness" by physiologically-patterned weak transcerebral magnetic fields: QEEG and source localization" Epilepsy & Behavior 28 (2013).

Persinger. "The neuropsychiatry of paranormal experiences". J Neuropsychiatry Clin Neurosci 2001.

Persinger. "Neuropsychological bases of god beliefs", New York: Praeger, 1987

Persinger. "Temporal lobe epileptic signs and correlative behaviors displayed by normal populations", Journal of General Psychology, 1986

Perry BD, Pollard R. Homeostasis, stress, trauma, and adaptation. A neurodevelopmental view of childhood trauma. Child Adolesc Psychiatr Clin N Am. 1998;7:33.

Paré, D. & Llinás, R. (1995), 'Conscious and preconscious processes as seen from the standpoint of sleep-waking cycle neurophysiology', Neuropsychologia, 33.

P. S. de Laplace. Essai Philosophique sur les Probabilites [1814], in Academy des Sciences, Oeuvres Complotes de Laplace, Vol. 7, Gauthier-Villars, Paris (1886).

Perrett DI, Harries MH, Bevan R, Thomas S, Benson PJ, Mistlin AJ, Chitty AJ, Hietanen JK, Ortega JE (1989) Frameworks of analysis for the neural representation of animate objects and actions. J Exp Bio 146: 87–113.

Phillips ML, Young AW, Senior C, Brammer M, Andrew C, Calder AJ, Bullmore ET, Perrett DI, Rowland D, Williams SC, Gray JA, David AS (1997) A specific neural substrate for perceiving facial expressions of disgust. Nature 389: 495–498.

Phillips ML, Young AW, Scott SK, Calder AJ, Andrew C, Giampietro V, Williams SC, Bullmore ET, Brammer M, Gray JA (1998) Neural responses to facial and vocal expressions of fear and disgust. Proc R Soc Lond B Biol Sci 265: 1809–1817.

Puce A, Perrett D (2003) Electrophysiological and brain imaging of biological motion. Philosoph Trans Royal Soc Lond, Series B, 358: 435–445.

Ramachandran VS. Behavioral and magnetoencephalographic correlates of plasticity in the adult human brain. Proc Natl Acad Sci USA 1993; 90: 10413–20.

Ramachandran VS. Phantom limbs, neglect syndromes, repressed memories, and Freudian psychology. Int Rev Neurobiol 1994; 37: 291–333.

Ramachandran VS. Plasticity and functional recovery in neurology. Clin Med 2005; 5: 368–73.

Ramachandran VS, Hirstein W. The perception of phantom limbs. The D. O. Hebb lecture. Brain 1998; 121: 1603–30.

Ramachandran VS, Rogers-Ramachandran D, Cobb S. Touching the phantom limb. Nature 1995; 377: 489–90.

Ramachandran VS, Rogers-Ramachandran D. Phantom limbs and neural plasticity. Arch Neurol 2000; 57: 317–20.

Ramachandran VS, Rogers-Ramachandran D. It's all done with mirrors. Sci Am Mind 2007; 18: 16–9.

Ramachandran VS, Rogers-Ramachandran D. Sensations referred to a patient's phantom arm from another subjects intact arm: perceptual correlates of mirror neurons. Med Hypotheses 2008; 70: 1233–4.

Ramachandran VS, Rogers-Ramachandran D, Stewart M. Perceptual correlates of massive cortical reorganization. Science 1992; 258: 1159–60.

Rizzolatti G, Craighero L (2004) The mirror-neuron system. Annu Rev Neurosci 27: 169–192.

Rizzolatti G, Fogassi L, Gallese V (2001) Neurophysiological mechanisms underlying the understanding and imitation of action. Nature Rev Neurosci 2:661–670.

Rock I, Victor J. Vision and touch: an experimentally created conflict between the two senses. Science 1964; 143: 594–6.

Rose´n B, Lundborg G. Training with a mirror in rehabilitation of the hand. Scand J Plast Reconstr Surg Hand Surg 2005; 39: 104–8.

Royet JP, Plailly J, Delon-Martin C, Kareken DA, Segebarth C (2003) fMRI of emotional responses to odors: influence of hedonic valence and judgment, handedness, and gender. Neuroimage 20: 713–728.

Rozin R Haidt J and McCauley CR (2000) Disgust. In: Lewis M, Haviland-Jones JM (eds) Handbook of Emotion. 2nd Edition. Guilford Press, New York, pp 637–653.

Saxe R, Carey S, Kanwisher N (2004) Understanding other minds: linking developmental psychology and functional neuroimaging. Annu Rev Psychol 55: 87–124.

S. J. Russell and P. Norvig, Artificial intelligence: a modern approach (3rd edition): Prentice Hall, 2009.

Schienle A, Stark R, Walter B, Blecker C, Ott U, Kirsch P, Sammer G, Vaitl D (2002) The insula is not specifically involved in disgust processing: an fMRI study. Neuroreport 13: 2023–2026.

Showers MJC, Lauer EW (1961) Somatovisceral motor patterns in the insula. J Comp Neurol 117: 107–115.

Singer T, Seymour B, O'Doherty J, Kaube H, Dolan RJ, Frith CD (2004) Empathy for pain involves the affective but not the sensory components of pain. Science 303: 1157–1162.

Smith A (1759) The theory of moral sentiments (ed. 1976). Clarendon Press, Oxford.

S. N. Bose (1924). "Plancks Gesetz und Lichtquantenhypothese". Zeitschrift für Physik. 26 (1): 178–181.

Sprengelmeyer R, Rausch M, Eysel UT, Przuntek H (1998) Neural structures associated with recognition of facial expressions of basic emotions Proc R Soc Lond B Biol Sci 265: 1927–1931.

Strafella AP, Paus T (2000) Modulation of cortical excitability during action observation: a transcranial magnetic stimulation study. NeuroReport 11: 2289–2292.

Simonsen R (2015) Eating for the future: veganism and the challenge of in vitro meat. In: Stapleton P, Byers A (Hg). Biopolitics and utopia. Palgrave Macmillan, New York (2015), S 167–190

Tanaka K (1996) Inferotemporal cortex and object vision. Ann Rev Neurosci. 19: 109–140.

Tesla N. "My Inventions", 1919

T. R. Society, "Machine learning: the power and promise of computers that learn by example," ed. The Royal Society, 2017.

Tomasello M, Call J (1997) Primate cognition. Oxford University Press, Oxford.

Tremblay C, Robert M, Pascual-Leone A, Lepore F, Nguyen DK, Carmant L, Bouthillier A, Theoret H (2004) Action observation and execution: intracranial recordings in a human subject. Neurology. 63: 937–938.

Umilta MA, Kohler E, Gallese V, Fogassi L, Fadiga L, Keysers C, Rizzolatti G (2001) "I know what you are doing": a neurophysiological study. Neuron 32: 91–101.

Von Wright G.H., (1963), Norm and Action. A Logical Inquiry, Routledge & Kegan Paul, London.

Von Wright G.H., (1976), "Determinism and the Study of Man", in Essays on Explanation and Understanding, ed. by J. Manninen and R. Tuomela, Reidel, Dordrecht.

Von Wright G.H., (1977), "What is Humanism?", The Lindlay Lecture, University of Arkansas, Lawrence, Kansas.

Von Wright G.H., (1979), "Humanism and the Humanities", in Philosophy and Grammar, ed. by S. Kanger and S. Öhman, Reidel, Dordrecht, pp. 1-16. Reprinted in von Wright (1993).

Von Wright G.H., (1980), Freedom and Determination, North-Holland Publishing Co., Amsterdam.

Von Wright G.H., (1985), Of Human Freedom, The Tanner Lectures on Human Values,

Vol. VI, ed. by S. M. McMurrin, University of Utah Press, Salt Lake City, pp. 107-70. Reprinted in von Wright (1998).

Von Wright G.H., (1993), The Tree of Knowledge and Other Essays, Brill, Leiden.

Von Wright G.H., (1997), "Progress: Fact and Fiction", in The Idea of Progress, ed. by A. Burgen et al., W. de Gruyter, Berlin, pp. 1-18.

Von Wright G.H., (1998), In the Shadow of Descartes: Essays in the Philosophy of Mind, Kluwer, Dordrecht.

NO FOREIGNER ONLY FAMILY

NO FOREIGNER ONLY FAMILY

NO FOREIGNER ONLY FAMILY